WHAT IS BLADING?

When you first get a pair of blades, the front door of your home becomes a doorway to another world. You will never see your surroundings in the same way again. Your first wobble on a pair of blades starts you on a quest to find the smoothest routes through the streets. Soon you're sweeping downhill or pulling radical airs.

Most people start blading with a gentle cruise around the park on a borrowed or rented pair of blades. But once you've mastered the basic blading skills, you'll find your pulse rate and your speed levels rising.

Blading Tech Talk

Hard boots – Similar in design to a ski boot, gives lots of support (good for beginners).

Soft boots – Boots made from soft trainer-type materials, advantages are that they're breathable, light and good to look at.

Frame – The part of the skate where the wheels are held.

Bearings – Tiny metal balls inside the wheels that help them to roll faster.

ABEC rating – Manufacturers give bearings a number to indicate how accurately they are made (higher number means more accurate, faster bearing).

Foot bed – Soft foam sheet that can be placed under the foot; installing a better one is the easiest way to improve any skate.

Bladers enjoying the sunshine.

4

The Four Kinds of Blading:

● **Recreational:** blading for fitness and fun.

● **Aggressive/street:** performing tricks and jumps on obstacles in skate parks or the street.

● **Hockey:** like ice hockey but on blades.

● **Speed:** blading as fast as you can downhill.

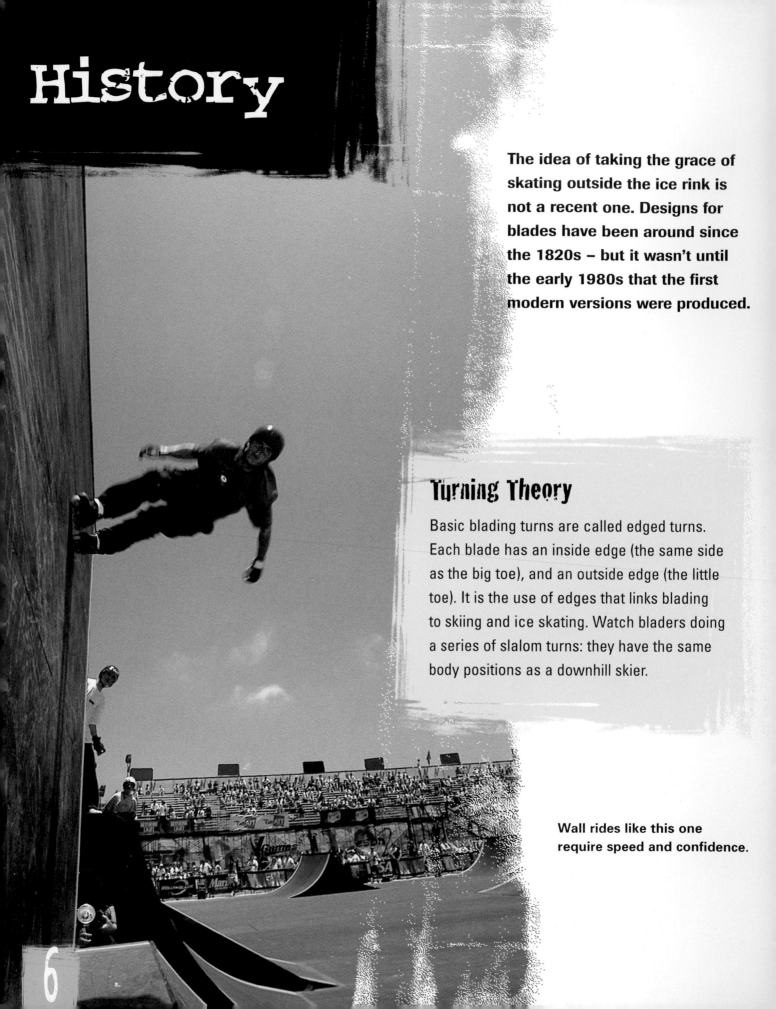

History

The idea of taking the grace of skating outside the ice rink is not a recent one. Designs for blades have been around since the 1820s – but it wasn't until the early 1980s that the first modern versions were produced.

Turning Theory

Basic blading turns are called edged turns. Each blade has an inside edge (the same side as the big toe), and an outside edge (the little toe). It is the use of edges that links blading to skiing and ice skating. Watch bladers doing a series of slalom turns: they have the same body positions as a downhill skier.

Wall rides like this one require speed and confidence.

Below: Pro skater Oli Short royales a wooden rail with a 10' drop in Manchester city centre, England.

Above: Bladers building their own mini-ramp.

Scott and Brennan Olson, two ice hockey players from Minneapolis, USA, used hockey-type boots, a rigid chassis and urethane wheels to make the first-ever blades. Before long, people all over the USA realised that wide, smooth walkways, particularly those of the coastal towns, were ideal places to blade. Skiers, ice skaters and hockey players appreciated the chance to do a similar sport outdoors in the summer sunshine. Other people caught on too, and soon blading spread to Europe and beyond.

Rough Riders

Early blades manufactured by people like Robert John Tyres were not hugely popular, probably because they had iron wheels!

Safety equipment is important for bladers. The amount of padding you wear should always reflect the worst-case scenario for the type of skating that you are doing. Even the most experienced bladers take a fall once in a while. Remember, when things go wrong on skates, they go wrong very quickly.

Minimum Requirements

Recreational blading

Wrists guards and knee pads (learners should add elbow pads and a helmet).

- - - - - - **Standard helmet**

Aggressive blading

Wrist guards; knee and elbow pads are much thicker than recreational pads, to spread the load of a fall from a great height; and helmet. Perhaps shin guards and a 'nappy' (a pair of padded shorts).

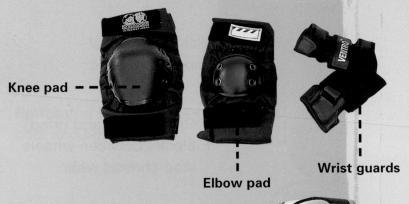

Knee pad - - - - - -

Elbow pad

Wrist guards

Hockey

Wrist, knee and elbow pads are the minimum. Hockey clubs will insist that bladers wear full protection during a game – upper and lower body armour, padded gloves, a face visor and gum shield.

Goalie's mask - - - - for hockey

Speed skating

The need to keep an aerodynamic shape means that padding is kept to a minimum. Wrist guards and a helmet are an essential requirement, but with just these an accident can be very dangerous.

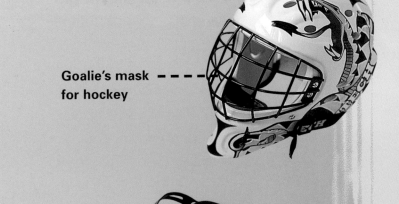

Wrist guards - - - -

Protection Guidelines

- No amount of protection is too much.
- Think about the skating that you will be doing, and imagine the type of accident that you may have.
- Get fully padded up before practising new moves.

BASIC techniques

Brake control is the hardest basic blading skill to learn. Your body's natural reaction when things start to go wrong is to tense up. This causes your knees to straighten and your head to pull back, which is the opposite of good braking technique. So, the first rule is to stay calm.

Heel braking

All beginner blades have a heel brake: this is a large rubber block at the back of one blade. There is more than one way to stop, but heel braking is the first method to learn because it's the easiest. More advanced ways of stopping, like the T-stop and the power slide, require advanced skills.

Slide the braking foot out in front of the supporting blade.

Lift your toe. When the brake is touching the floor, bend your knees. The weight of your hips slows you down.

Keep everything – knees, shoulders and head – forward. Stretching your arms straight out in front will bring even more weight forward.

Top Tip

If you are worried about putting blades on for the very first time, make use of the anti-rolling properties of carpet. When wearing blades on carpet you'll be able to walk around and get a feel for the weight of the blades. When you feel confident, move outside.

Try to keep the braking foot out in front. If you let it slip back alongside your supporting foot you will not stop.

The power slide braking technique needs a lot of balance and good edge control. Practise blading on one foot and backwards to obtain the skills needed.

AGGRESSIVE skating

Alex Jones balances an alley-oop soul on this steep down ledge in California, USA.

You don't have to be aggressive to be an aggressive skater! But aggressive bladers do have a different attitude to their sport. To experienced aggressive bladers, the urban environment is an adventure park, full of wild rides. Stairs, rails, curbs and benches are not obstacles but opportunities for tricks and grinds.

The move that sets aggressive blading apart from all other styles is the grind. Grinds can be performed on curbs, benches, handrails – anything that will slide on a part of the skate. Remember, though: if it's hard enough to grind, it's hard enough to hurt. When learning aggressive skating it's especially important to wear a helmet, because the back of your head is very exposed if you fall backwards.

Grind Terms

Alley-oop – Any grind performed backwards.

Backside – Turn 90 degrees to the left.

Backslide – Grindng on the edge of your back foot while grabbing the front foot.

Frontside grind – With the rail on your right, turn 90 degrees to the right when you jump on to it.

Sole grind – Front foot across the rail, rear foot in line with the rail sliding on the outside sole of the boot.

Unity – Feet crossed as you slide down the rail.

Albert Hooi holds a Unity grind
on Weymouth seafront, England.

Spaniard, Enanoh Moreno makes his mark on
the UK with this misfit grind in Brighton.

Empty car parks are a skaters playground.
Tom Penfound backslides this ledge in
Manchester, England.

Mike Welland holds a fishbrain through a curved
ledge in Liverpool city centre, England.

Getting Air

Jumping, or 'getting air', is a basic skill that all aggressive bladers need to master. To start with, you will get air when you jump on and off a grind rail, but leaving the ground is only the start of getting air. Spins, flips and grabs give extra style to tricks, and in competitions big, stylish airs score more points.

How to Air.

1 Place the ramp somewhere with plenty of space. Start by rolling up to the ramp very slowly and turning on the ramp. Roll out facing back the way you came.

2 Next, roll in with enough speed to take you up to the lip and roll out backwards ('fakie'). These moves will familiarise you with the feel of the ramp.

3 Skate to the ramp with plenty of speed and 'pop' up as you reach the lip. 'Popping' means straightening your knees and is basically a small jump.

4 Bend your knees and keep your weight forward for the landing. Roll out from the landing.

5 Look out for obstacles like lampposts: you may be travelling quite fast!

16

Big Air

The official world record for getting air on blades is 2.7 metres, by Raphael Sandoz of Switzerland.

17

SKATE parks

The skate park is the safest place to learn aggressive skating, meet other people who are into the same kind of skating and see new manoeuvres.

Trick Terms

Fakie – Any trick done backwards.

Grab – Holding skates during a trick.

Bio – A sideways spin performed while horizontal.

Mute – Grabbing the opposite skate with your arm going across the front of your body.

Late – Tricks performed closer to landing, which score more respect.

When you first enter a skate park it seems like complete chaos. There are people grinding and pulling airs all over the place. But, there is order in the disorder and it pays to hang back for a while to see what is going on. Park Life Rules (right) will help you figure it out.

Park Life Rules

- If you are waiting beside a top skater, let them have their run first.

- Make sure that you get your turn, when it is your turn.

- Keep your eyes open and try not to stand in anyone's way.

- Try not to cross other people's paths.

- Enjoy the place and the vibe – everyone (including you) has a right to be there.

Mini ramp

A smaller version of the vert ramp, usually about 2 metres high and definitely the place to start.

Street course

Usually the largest area of the park. Around the edge are hips, quarter pipes and roll-ins. In the middle are fun boxes and rails.

Vert ramp

The big half pipe can be anything from 2.5 to 4.5 metres top to bottom; not for the faint hearted.

Competitions

Aggressive skate competitions are fun for bladers of all abilities. Competitors see them as a chance to find out how good they really are. For spectators, competitions are places to meet old friends and keep up with the latest tricks and fashions. For sponsors, they are the perfect places to have their products seen and identified with success.

What to Expect at a Competition:

1 Turn up and register. You will be given a number.

2 Your number will be called with about 20 other bladers for a 20-minute street-skating practice session.

3 When everyone has practised, qualifying runs will be held.

4 Those who qualify will then skate two runs of one minute each in the final.

5 After the street competition has finished there will probably be a mini-ramp comp and a vert comp.

6 All the scores are counted and a winner is announced for each section. The winners are showered with prizes and products from sponsors.

Getting a sponsor

Doing well in competitions is the best way to attract a sponsor's attention, but not the only way. Getting on with other bladers and practising hard are other ways to attract the interest of sponsors. It's not just big manufacturers who sponsor bladers; your local skate shop might also be a source of sponsorship.

Indoor and undercover competitions can go ahead whatever the weather.

Top Five Heroes

- Arlo Eisenberg (USA)
- Jon Julio (USA)
- Chris Edwards (USA)
- Chris Haffey (USA)
- Rene Hulgreen (Denmark)

21

American Jeff Stockwell performs a vertical soul stall deep in Mexico.

Street skating is the original form of aggressive blading. Indoor skate parks are good places to hold competitions and to use blades when the rain is pouring, but some bladers are never seen there. These are the hard-core street skaters.

As well as the skills needed to do 'sick' tricks, street bladers also have to deal with problems like bad weather, traffic and the general public. There are no judges to please; the pleasures of street skating are pure fun and the respect of other bladers.

5 All-Time Classic Blading DVDs

- *The Hoax 2*
- *E2F*
- *VG3*
- *Damaged Goods*
- *The Adventures of Mr Moosenuckle*

22

Rawlinson Rivera is picked out by the camera's flash.

London ripper, Leon Humphries floats a mute air
for the passing bus at the Clockwork Orange banks.

Street Survival Kit

Things to have in your rucksack:

- Some antiseptic plasters.

- Shoes and, if possible, a mobile
  phone.

- Take plenty of fluid, especially
  if the sun is out or it's hot.

- A couple of spare bearings: if a
  bearing disintegrates while you
  are out, it can ruin a session.

- A blade tool. These combine
  allen keys, bearing pushers
  and any number of other
  useful tools.

- Take cab fare. If you take a big
  slam, you might not feel like
  skating home.

Pioneers
and heroes

Arlo Eisenberg

Despite having been one of the pioneers of aggressive blading in the 1980s, Arlo still skates at a high level.

Arlo Eisenberg

One of the all-time great pioneers of aggressive skating is Arlo Eisenburg. Together he and Chris Edwards were among the very first people to skate in a style that had more to do with skateboarding than ice skating. Arlo adapted his skates so that he could perform grinds, and was one of the first bladers to be into jumps and airs.

Chris Edwards

Chris Edwards started blading when he was 13. At first he skated near his home in Escondido, USA, but was soon signed-up to skate for Team Rollerblade. 'I just wanted someone else to ride with,' he says. The first in-line competitions were anything but competitive – Chris won them all. He excels on the big half pipe; at his best, he amazed judges with his massive, contorted airs. Having once said, 'I will skate forever', he is still regularly placed in the top ten at competitions.

Jon Julio

Jon Julio has been inspiring generations of bladers since 1995. He has invented countless tricks like the unity, backslide and topside acid. Along with a successful pro career, Jon's been involved with clothing companies, wheel manufacturers and he has even founded the street competition, IMYTA. Jon continues to push the sport with innovative video sections and his own skate brand.

One of blading's founding fathers, Jon Julio, is still innovating with tricks like this vertical top acid stall to fakie in Manchester.

ROLLER Hockey

Blades were born out of the ice hockey scene, so it is no surprise that hockey is still part of the sport of blading. The rules of the game are based on ice hockey, with a few adjustments. Any blader with a basic knowledge of how to skate can play hockey. Two of the all-time greats of the NHL, Wayne Gretzky and Brett Hull, promoted blading as an accompaniment to playing ice hockey.

A fully padded roller hockey player.

Club Hockey Rules

- Mandatory protection: helmet, elbow pads, gloves, kneepads, shin guards and gum shield. Goalkeepers require extra protection.

- No charging, tripping or roughing.

- No holding on to feet, hands or sticks.

- No interfering with a player who doesn't have the puck.

Pucks.

Glove.

Stick.

Standard helmet (Goalie's
helmet shown on page 10).

Knee and
shin guard.

Chest and
shoulder padding.

Basic Knockabout Hockey Requirements

- Normal recreational skating kit (see page 8).

- One stick per player.

- A crushed drinks can, to use as a puck.

Ethics and Quiz

Blading is a fun sport, and it should be carried out with a smile. When skating around other people, remember that the reason that there are relatively few rules to follow is because everyone tries to get on with each other. Give everyone around you the respect that they deserve. As you become more experienced, remember how you felt when you were a beginner and try to give a bit of help to people who are just taking up the sport.

You are blading behind a crowd of pedestrians, do you?

A: Shout, so that they move out of your way.

B: Push them gently to one side.

C: Slow down and follow behind until you can pass safely.

While blading you find yourself at the top of a hill that is much steeper than you can deal with. Do you?

A: Keep going and sort out any problems later.

B: Stop and put on more protection.

C: Stop and remove your skates.

You see a beginner having problems, do you?

A: Stop and laugh.

B: Turn up your personal stereo.

C: Stop and give some advice.

How did you do?

Mostly A: You should consider taking up meditation rather than blading.

Mostly B: You have the right idea but you should work on your inter-personal skills.

Mostly C: You will be an asset to the blading scene – blade in peace.

Glossary

Word:	Means:	Dosen't Mean:
Air	A jump performed on blades.	Stuff you breathe.
Bearings	Tiny metal balls that allow wheels to spin more freely.	Positional guides.
Cruise	Gentle blading session, taking your time to get from one place to the next.	Holiday on board ship.
Edged	Describes a turn that uses the edges of the wheels.	Moved cautiously along a narrow ledge.
Fakie	Describes any trick done while moving/rolling backwards.	Pretender.
Grind	A trick in which the frame of the blade is used to slide along a wall's corner or a hand rail, for example.	Pulverise.
Half pipe	A large, steep, double-sided ramp on which bladers (and skateboarders and BMXers) perform tricks.	Broken drain.
Heel brake	A block of soft, rubbery plastic on the heel of a blade , which allows bladers to slow down.	Fracture bone in heel.
Power slide	An advanced braking technique (see page 13 for a photo).	Loss of power.
T-stop	An advanced braking technique, where the blader drags his or her foot sideways to slow down.	Rest for cuppa.

Further Information

Books

No Limits: In-line Skating Jed Morgan,
Watts (2005)

X Sports: Agressive In-line Skating
Anne Weil, Edge Books (2004)

Internet

www.kingdom-mag.co.uk
The website for Kingdom Magazine
is packed with the latest information
plus video and sound clips and loads
of photos.

www.aggressive.com
Log on to this website for the latest prod-
uct reviews, skills and top tips, plus
videos and photos.

World Records

World 1-hour record: In Feb 1991, Eddy Matzger (USA), at Long Beach, California, skated 34.82 kms in 1 hour.

World 12-hour record: In Feb 1991, Jonathan Seutter (USA), at Long Beach, California, skated 285.86 kms in 12 hours.

Longest Railslide: In June 2002, Chris Haffey slid 202.9 m on a Los Angeles handrail (unofficial record).

Index

Picture Acknowlegements
The publishers would like to thank the
following for giving their permission for
photos to be used in this book: page14,
15, 20, 21(b), 22, 23(b) 25 Joe Coyne -
Editor of Kingdom Magazine; all other
photos supplied by Ben Roberts.